The Diener

Barataria Poetry

AVA LEAVELL HAYMON
SERIES EDITOR

The Diener

POEMS

Martha Serpas

LOUISIANA STATE UNIVERSITY PRESS
BATON ROUGE

Published by Louisiana State University Press
Copyright © 2015 by Martha Serpas
Manufactured in the United States of America
LSU Press Paperback Original
First printing

DESIGNER: Michelle A. Neustrom
TYPEFACE: Sina Nova

LIBRARY OF CONGRESS
CATALOGING-IN-PUBLICATION DATA

Serpas, Martha.
  [Poems. Selections]
  The diener : poems / Martha Serpas.
    pages cm — (Barataria poetry)
    ISBN 978-0-8071-5922-4 (pbk. : alk. paper) —
ISBN 978-0-8071-5923-1 (pdf) — ISBN 978-0-8071-
5924-8 (epub) — ISBN 978-0-8071-5925-5 (mobi)
    I. Title.
    PS3619.E77A6 2015
    811'.6—dc23

                                          2014025259

For Harold

CONTENTS

The Diener

The Diener

We hated the early anatomists
for showing us how fragile we are,
how God's image is composite:
the liver the bright bruise of a sunset,
the thyroid wrapped around our throats
for luck. They saw our brains folded
against our foreheads and knew our hearts
pump dumbly on through the wash.
And wily guts take the brunt of it,
pushing to get rid of while we insist
on taking in and taking in and taking in.
Theirs was heresy, that is, a choice
to reach the Artist by testing the art,
human suffering always the requisite cost.

Change, what keeps all of it the same,
the Teacher says, no new thing
under the sun. What we make, let's make old
instead, older than the first tool,
which smelled much like the body—
the first blacksmith must have thought—
not quite like displaced blood, but blood at home
in its place among other parts in their places,
and that must be how we began to confuse
the power to examine and change
with the power to create, to be discrete agents,
why we like to see ourselves as whole,
despite the diener piling legs on a cot,
despite the pruned artery, tied and cut.

Betsy

Without my vigil, it happens. Bright green fern,
    humeral veil of ordinary time,

covers these crossed oak branches as if
    the sky is too holy for wood to touch.

In the dry days before, I admire
    the cracked bark and dark brown color

of my eyes and hair, the resistance
    I lack, the wisdom the wind brings every

hurricane season.   September 9th,
    1965, I waited like a reef

in my mother's womb, listening to small
    branches crack and rain land insistent

against the drumming clapboard, a bedroom
    window finally giving in. I could breathe

the rising water, fire ants, a used-up
    black moccasin less patient

with the erratic tide than I.
    The only levee between me and

the known seething world was flesh and regret,
    and beyond, the silver wash hiding

the familiar. Men would come much later,
    sinking their shoulders and shovels

into the soft land, the uninhibited water.
    And because the mud peels open for them,

they think they have won. Their high places become
    low places again. Single-minded. Graceful.

God, how I want to tell you this story!
    The plywood goes up from inside,

as it must, nailed to the frame, the wind banned
    from what's left of the house, and everyone

exhales and shakes their wet clothes, except me
    who's been drenched and naked, carefree,

for months in the uterine undertow,
    or maybe beyond months, belonging to

a steady thought (not mine) that repeats itself,
    one that won't translate to resurrection.

Sunshine Bridge

MISSISSIPPI RIVER CROSSING
ASCENSION PARISH, LOUISIANA

Not quite in the middle of the joint, of course,
    but close enough, strides the big bronze River,

Inked with barges and tugboats and flexed
    like Popeye's forearms between two engines.

It unzips the country or cinches it,
    insatiable drunk, always heading back

To South Pass thick with spoil and swill. To
    hurdle that snoring body, we must drive

West to go east, north to go south, glinting
    St. Christophers on the dash, our radios

Playing, *You are my sunshine… you make me
    happy when skies are gray.*

That's why I'll always be around… If it's Friday
    we make the Way of the Cross—

Two JD and Cokes, chilled Southern Comfort, and
    a Bloody Mary for my Baptist friend,

Who toasts the asphalt for what it's really saying,
    You only think you're getting somewhere.

All trussed up toward the edge of the earth
    then saved at the last by a steel suspension.

≈≈

O Span to Brooklyn, everybody's have to have, you homebody.
      Everyone can see you there squatting.

I can't love you, your bricks right there, strong-arming
      the shore and never getting fat.

Tall cerise ship, too aloof and
      graceful to bag the wind, too busy anointing

Herself with the sky. And still everybody gawks.
      No, I'm crossing plaits of cane,

Chemical plants and neutral grounds
      dividing nothing. I'm getting to

Crossroads without signs and cane trucks
      without lights. I can't tell you

How to get here from wherever you are.
      Just let me say the sun shines everywhere,

On the just and unjust, and, yes, on Westminster, and
      sometimes at an angle on the River.

You think he might be bronze after all,
      that old blowhard. Who wouldn't

Want barges on big forearms like gnats
      in July? Who wouldn't want to be a shining

Hill on a bridge, a bridge to the east of nowhere,
    right at the center of the vanishing

Of every end and start, of mileage unthreading,
    of exits, of the mind's highest point?

Pearl Snap

Education *is* the answer
to our social woes, and not
the get-a-good-job-after-high-school,
but the deep plodding kind, the making-
of-many-books kind, get-everybody-
together-to-debate-the-big-questions

kind. When I'm in Walmart
and some kid dangling by the wrist
is screaming, his mom in shorts that
slice her thighs saying something
deep to him through her teeth,
her long hair smelling like she has

more than one job, I know it's not her fault.
She's carrying a combination wallet/
cigarette case with a pocket for the lighter.
Her husband—well, the father of her last two,
her divorce isn't final from her ex—
is waiting in the truck, a Ford. Her dad

had a problem with *that* until they went
duck hunting and worked it
all out. Her man didn't graduate
even though his junior high let
the boys go when trawling season
began, but going back got harder.

She took typing and bookkeeping
and even AP math. She says she manages
a convenience store, where you learn
how to just take on the present.
Right now she just needs
to find that pearl snap for her oldest

and why is it suddenly so dang hard
to find a boy's twelve pearl snap?
They're a few like her in every cow town.
When the copter brings a woman's
child—a certain woman of that kind—
from the parish or the county

to the city, and we all stand around
the trauma bay watching environmental services
sweep up the gauze wrap and cut clothes,
and that woman from the boonies
is *still* not here, driving her husband's
truck as hard and steady as she can,

I'll meet her in family consult
or stand her in the shiny hallway—
she'll go anywhere—and depending
on what the test tube intern has to say,
she'll either squat, lay her forearm
against her stomach, and loose

that first wail-groan that defies conceit,
or she'll tutor me in the language
of living in good faith, of staring
down what I have to say and
opening her mind to it, taking
it in like a nursling and knowing it

whole until the two can sleep side by side.
We tell her, *it's gonna be a long road,* and
she says, *as long as there's a road, I'm on it.*

Badlands

All over his body wolves send up a mad
        chorus to the moon

seeping green
        across his arms and his chest

and where his new liver floats up in him
        like a mushroom's flat cap.

"I feel like I'm tripping," he says
        at a pitch lower than his wife hears,

and then "and I don't believe in God."
        No room in that room.

So much white. So much blue.
        The wolves cry the great name

into the hallway where a gurney
        rolls up and down the tile

looking for someone to play catch with.
        Push the wheels straight, pull the cot—

it's my job to take the heat of belief.
        On Wednesday

the nurses line up for ashes
        in their white Crocs

and Reeboks. Wolfman
        wants God so bad

he tattoos not-God—what seems not-God—
    on his skin, wants to tell me

he's afraid, that the room squeezes
    time like flexible hose,

that he forgets his wife's voice,
    that men come in the night

to argue with him about the nature
    of stars. There are puddles of stars above

the silver wolves on his chest. Not-God sets
    a chair near his bed.

He says thank you and lays
    a hand on the skinny arm

and with his moist stare and rough
    face tries to convey

how much he trusts the moon
    who centers the persistent stars

and how he forgets the soldier sun
    who keeps everyone blinking and quiet.

Breakfast at Starbucks with Egret

Don't think less of me, Reader.
In years to come, I am confident,
a footnote will be necessary.
But newspapers will still accompany
coffee and poets will smoke
two-for-one cigarettes
over curled yellow pads
wherever the former are sold.

We saw, as we herded ourselves through the slot
of the drive-thru, a cattle egret
standing aside the mini-mike and menu,
noble and goofy as a stuffed giraffe.
Into the crotons it went
and snatched up a lizard in the straw
of its beak, belly-held it for a beat
before tossing it down
like popcorn. "Dinner for a week!"

my friend said to her frappé
just before the white-crested glutton swallowed
another appendage waving green.

Consider the egrets of the parking lot.

Consider you and me saying goodbye
over a two-pump mocha
and the plain dark roast that will suffice.

Hirudo Medicinalis

It is hard to be misunderstood.
And how many of us get vindication
after a century or so?

I mistook the little bloodsucker
for a wad of gauze as it whirled
from the sailor's spliced thumb.

It became an iridescent helix,
a liquid amber's leaf
dangling through a day-long

spring and fall and spring.
Have you ever taken God's name
in vain? Forgotten all your Latin

but *opiate* and *parasite,* believe
it's God who eats at our table?
The sailor calls his savior Fat Albert.

"C'mon, there you go," he soothes.
"Fix me all over, fix my heart, fix everything
around me." What carries us forward,

when I enter the room,
is the blankness—the sheets,
the walls, the page.

Language itself is prophylactic.
It avails us, suspends the hours
for us, inscribes our intentions,

seams the ordinary, provides
for the whiting in which, in this case,
the sailor and I can make our poem.

His poem is about wholeness and joy.
Mine is about the illusion of linear
progress, about Albert spinning

his symbiotic segments as he waits
in his salty pyx, both host and communicant,
the three of us chanting the same poem.

Free Descent

i
It seemed I had always been kicking
in the fringing reefs, fiddling with my breathing
to find a buoyancy I thought was neutral.

Don't get me wrong: there was charm
          to the coral coliseum, light curling
right to left on the golden vase sponges.

Mostly I had been holding my depth gauge
in front of my mask like a railroad watch,
                              a needle

telling me where I had to be, my hand opening
          too soon for the anchor line.

ii
Today I am rolling into spangled

blue with no air in my vest. I've quit signing
OK. I am not equalizing, inflating,

adjusting, or looking for my buddy.
I drop like windswept rain over glass.
A stowaway on a blue exhale.

This is the wall of my free descent.
                    Extravagant sound

and bright flourishes, annunciating
anemones flaring like Roman

candles. Sea fans swaying
            in a last red trace

past nothing I am owed or owe.

iii
A satin ball, huge as Saturn, hangs
from the lowest branch. I reach

for its crescent lights and it falls,
                    sickles spinning.

Red tentacles spill from my fingertip
        into a waterfall, the chrome, the porcelain glowing.

Lesson: Wonder precedes and postpones pain.

iv
The tangs and triggers wave
from their convertibles. The peppermint wrasse

hides and reappears, tilts and twirls, comical.
                            Around them
skillet fish flash like dimes in a gumball machine,
pop up and vanish into slick, chromatic sheens.

A spotted moray lurches purple and black

but doesn't bite, skirts the whorls of tender pink
shells then disappears into the mind's blue cup.

v

Only a dream, I was told: the water
rising around the legs of my high chair,
tin cans stacked like doubloons.

First the water swallowed
the linoleum, the baseboards
then the cat's red dish, the teetering blinds.

vi

I once dived along the platform's algae-
　　　shaped legs thick as a lady's stockings.

Spearfishers, sharp barnacles,
a sudden chop, all dangerous
in the confines of the rig.

A mobile of lookdowns
in a glowing white thermocline.
Above us a buoy sounding steady
　　　as an artificial heart.

vii

No quiet like inescapable quiet.

viii

Demand. Valve. Draw. Pull. Hold.
Her mouth seals my mouth.
Her body seals my body.

I am so full, inside the trees,
in the field, on a child's bed,
I break elemental.
            I beat the lungs. I free flow.

A silence behind the staircase
                    where only souls can fit.

ix
The disk of sunlight at the surface
is less a roof than the wide rim

of a bottomless shot glass, or the spinning
jeweled ballet of a mirrored box.

My body falls, an effervescence,
a threaded streamer, a thought about to sleep.

How could I miss what remains above me?

And here where the light passes off—
a green sea turtle, no longer clumsy

on the hard shore, wrangling with a trawl,
or bobbing bloated on the surface,

dives under me. How little we have
to say to each other, how its limbs move

for mine. Today I drop past the jellyfish's
giant ghosts into a black mouth, a bliss.

Sliding deeper, not to see the stars
again, but to fall and release the fall.

My smallest bubble rises on its own string
and narcosis with it, beginning.

Arrow Boy

They see her as a genie in a pager.
      They don't know how she was dreaming
in the Sleep Room, the Serenity Prayer—

the whole thing, not the AA clip—
      taped next to the phone, next to the clock,
next to the Bible, next to the Qur'an,

under the loose vent ticking shut, falling
      then rising again. A shredded Styrofoam cup,
a futile fold of paper caught in the gap.

Outside isolation, she wraps herself in green
      booties, gown, a mask spreading
her breath back over her lips and chin,

laminated wings, small as etched coins.
      When she crosses the fallen ward
toward the falling boy, his parents are waiting,

rubbing the fluorescence from their temples and eyes.
      They think someone is here, that something
will happen, but she has arrived to bring

the nothing happening to the something
      that is, a boy with a washcloth between his legs
and an arrow's vane splitting his mother

and his father to either side of his head.
      His flesh beads as if he is running hard,
a plastic fan swinging like a searchlight. And

she thinks he might want to talk to her,
        if he could, tell her how the point came
flying from its string, from his hand

to his brow—why should he speak to her,
        his throat free from the vent,
his eyes calculating the angles of draft?

And she's sorry to see the tube go. Soon he'll tuck
        his arms to his body like tiny wings, his chest
caving, his toes touching like a baby's.

His hand reminds her of a high school boy
        and his Escape cologne. After their dates
she didn't bathe and slept with her nose tucked

in her hand. Arrow Boy's lungs soar on their own
        over the helipad and the baler on the farm,
over his metallic Mustang where just last week

he was doing his girlfriend in the front seat,
        her thigh sending the volume screaming,
the music, the light from the dome, shooting out,

speeding into a dark that did not exist
        in a town full of steeples and shocks.
Even now, they think, the Lord could

unwrap him from himself, peel back his
        forehead and free the arrow with His hand.
Her prayers, they think, will complete

their faith "despite the thing they done that got
        their boy this hurt." Dad thinks his leaving launched the shaft.
Or was it Mom's remarriage? Should she pray *God's will*

or recite the assurance of Paul? *Neither death,*
        nor life, nor angels, nor principalities,
nor powers, nor things present, nor things to come,

can separate us from the love of God.
        The boy is already the guardian of this message.
She knows he will have to be starved,

his soul drawn out like egg whites from their shells.
        His mother is ready. His father still barters.
And she sees the boy rise on invisible scapulars,

already looking at the old couple as if they were strangers
        and at the woman holding their hands, she
an envelope's torn seal blown back behind the door.

The Wild Carp

What murky horrors must choke the wild carp
under the glass-grooved river

so that it shoots up, sliding through the green
light in a crazy arced radius—

catching the wind in its mouth
like a dog hanging out of a truck

its tags like so many scales
of refracted sun—

and even falling backwards toward the muck
rejoices with an exuberant slap

so that those of us paused on the bank
turn toward what we think we have missed

as if the fish had only one chain of joy
and its heroic life had just begun

Crossing

Out on the open water, finally, they see all
      seven deltas and their depositions,
mouth bars and inlets

running like childhood scars across the coast.

All night while the shrimp run
      and into the next hot day,
the last generation sits on Igloos

picking shrimp, following those before them
      till the nets are empty, passing the time
coaxing loggerheads close while bored porpoises

drift, with no wake to spin.

A certain quiet fills the hull
      for a proper discernment
of the shore, a certain sweat while they scan

for the new order of things,
      which is the old order renewed, things

moving swiftly but weighed immovable
      in their eyes. Someone might forget
to declare "good" or "very good" or "evil"

as they drift among their last breaths, their burials,
      and this third idle death that frees the soul's
wisdom, still ignorant of its crossing.

Who knows what God will breathe out
        after our last breath is drawn?

Some might see estuaries that unite
        the brackish bath and fluvial birth,
sandy islands that split the tide,

cypresses both grasping the bank and stretching
        their slender shadows on the channel

when God remembers the interstice
        of our muddy ossuary and our exhalations—
cordgrass and bulrush, bulltongue
and shellfish, sawgrass and maidencane—

a white coast of grass and salt and dragonflies.

Friends: Don't seal me in a marble card catalog
        to which no borrowers come.
Let the ferry go without me. Let me join
        the trawlers and gather my broad nets alone.

Aunt Kate Considers the Family Vault

THIBODAUX, LOUISIANA

She doesn't want to get dropped
     into the concrete vault below
the family tomb, and she doesn't

want to flip her brother Vincent
     either, onto her mother's bobby-pinned
hair, or her father's bones, both snapped

into silence. One could, one might escape
     one's parents' rousing echoes
above ground, tucked behind a catalog of

gray-green epitaphs like some blurry tattoo
     a laser could remove. She might
need that body when Jesus comes.

The Gulf might suck her out the grave
     and she'd be right there all glory
like a white robe clean out of the baptistry,
like a holy roller making a fuss.

White Dog

I do not recognize her as beautiful
but lost, a pin curl on my neighbor's

curb, of an uncertain age, too cold
for a winter in the South.

Someone, I think, should hold her.
Her eyes are brown, a swollen joint

where she's settled for pavement.
I throw a comforter over her. When

if ever should compassion be finite?
When I give her food, she buries it.

She wedges her head between
the pickets of my iron fleur-de-lis.

At 1 a.m. I am afraid to touch her.
She is quiet, denying she is caught.

I dig her a graceful exit, neither
of us admit I am helping her.

Sometimes she startles my face
with a quick lick, flings

a stuffed raccoon above her head
and laughs. I want her to be warm,

but not in my house. Soon she is next
to me in her La-Z-Boy, clawing

at my arm. She falls asleep, then
shuffles around in the morning.

I hear her Dearfoams dragging
the hardwoods. She comes to look

at me in bed, to see if I've made coffee.
No chance she'll trot out for the paper

herself. No one gets up. I put the water on
and after another nudge I let the dog out.

Settled on a Sunday

I love the boys, wherever they are,
because you loved them first.

I distrust them—even now—
because you loved them first.

Behind me the lemons pull
on the green branches

and the Spanish moss, so much
like our years, nearly touches

the ground. Why does the earth
move me so much

when I know it will take me
straight down naked

like a mangrove and unlike
a fig tree's binding roots

that hold the clay and rock,
and shoot green fruit

in summer for you to dry
on a windowsill

and bite into as if it had just
been snapped off the tree?

Sunset Limited

The Sunset Limited stops at Shriever
along LA 20 through the Chacahoula swamp

Sundays Tuesdays Fridays at seven and ten.
A century after the storm

the air dishes rotten pecans,
wet porches, a maimed screen door.

The road's the color of blood boudin
and potholes. Bald cypress, strands of moss.

At night the blackness
clings and presses like the best ride

at Pontchartrain Beach
for a scaredy-cat like me.

A bare-boned hand reached adagio
over the bitten balcony and shingled

cypress peaks of the Haunted House, then *bam,*
its spring-hinged doors sealed us to our howls.

I don't recall trick mirrors
or a cradling ghost, just black lights

and the day the park went bust.
Pay One Price, our inked wrists said,

and we did, raking the whole park
twice, late for the bus and not really lost

as we'd said.   That apportioned time
never looped on running rails

the way the banked and brazen Zephyr
pushed north then south to its fate.

I'm trying hard to see where I've gone.
With no fog lines on the shoulder,

it'd be easier to walk the old tracks
than drive this feeling of not coming back.

Ten Fathom Ledge

All that's visible
        is a ribbon of coral,
briny phrasals above a ledge nearly

erased by silt and scalloped water,
        ghostly and opaque.

Beyond is the dead outer shelf,
its tragic red surge of blossoms
        bruising the abyss.

What to do?
        The others have entered

the freighter's wrenched hull,
their light beams sliding like opera gloves
along the awkward deck and sides.

I am left playing with goatfish
        on Ten Fathom Ledge, the forbidden
step off your grandmother's porch,
the first plank as far as you will go
toward the long bright yard, the pitch
        of children rippling from a swing.

Why not be content with spadefish and nurse sharks,
        the confusion of gravity, the wise bezel
that grasps all our time as bottom time?
A gentle surge toward the wreck lifts, pauses,
        then sloshes me right back on the ledge.

≈≈

Everything lasts forever: the jetties,
        sand, sky, pipers, even the pebbles
of sea glass, cobalt, old as lace
doilies. Others can walk down the beach
toward thin shacks and driftwood shelters,
toward haze and mist. I'll sit on an unclaimed
        log, which has drifted here, for now,
and watch a midday sun crystal
on the waves. Don't be fooled:

The Gulf is not a polished cruiser
        or a V-hull on the dock.

The Gulf
        is not a flatiron idling
between sets of bowing waves.

Its striated water lifts itself inch by inch
and closes in on the shore.
                It is alive,
playing its chords, humming its undertow.

You will be welcomed on your back
as it slides its dress collar over
        your thighs, runs its breezes and tensions
all over you. It will welcome your face floating down,
closed eyes or open, as it breathes
        August's strong sweat.
It will welcome you a thousand times.
It wants you to practice sinking
            and feel how much you belong.

Others can walk the shore's silver brocade
        and pace back again.

Don't be fooled: The sky is complicit.
        There's no discerning compass here.
The wings and water pull equally
        toward the beauty of transparence—
        cirri, sea fans, music, love

and the pans and stirrups of pelicans
which weigh that anything is possible,
        but that nothing has to be.

Humus

Thank God it's rained enough to flood the streets
and slow water has settled on vacant lots,
      filled the low places.

The students choose their steps among
      the bumps and grasses,
veiling their heads with notes and paper bags.

And the high places, thank God,
      heralded in their green collars—

the live oak tops, I mean—are rivered far
      from my heretical reach.

Some mercurochromed boy scuffled up there
      and praised his own hands and knees,

marking the bark with his tread and
      wedging his feet between trunk and limbs,

his bare head turned up to the sun
      and its portico of wet bark and rain.

Neither of us knows the word *hubris,*
only the word *ground,* the center of the center

of a swamp where I stand
      worshiping the selfless boy

who climbs at will, twisting his corduroy
    frame down the ship rope and dropping his heels

on the low places that hum with fullness
    and splash into smoky crowns of brown light.

Asperges

Sudden summer rain, warm on my back
      like asperges slashes,
more of a blessing than anything

to get dolloped in the eye and laugh away
      the shame of believing
in any kind of redemptive wash

to get to the glass door before the stoup of sky
      spills, to be the chaplain
carrying in the far side of the walls.

Such an inconvenience to bring an umbrella
      in through the ER
best to leave these skinny hands free,

too much weather for environmental
      services to mop up
under cots and toddlers with their foil balloons.

≈≈

It's impossible not to ask *how ya doin'*?
      in the elevator for
the badge says I have to care, and for

three floors I do. Then for three minutes I talk
      to a nurse washing a big
baby boy whose green skin sloughs off

like bruised fruit skins. He died before any eye
          saw his angry face. And Job wished
for this? To move straight from womb to grave?

Or was it perfect immersion he sought,
          to soak between his mother's arms
suspended in pink-green marble

for weeks his mother either knowing or not
          knowing. Theirs could be no
broken, track-lit, eternal pietà.

≈≈

The jaundiced patient sleeps in a white sponge,
          drying out, her husband
entranced, two quarters between his fingers.

Best to leave both hands free for hoisting her head
          without spilling the coins and
for fetching Purell, which kills everything:

every body's soupy human smell, the scent
          of blood and grimy dust-mixed rain
on scrubs and button downs.

≈≈

A den of comforters in ICU waiting:
          fig newtons and pajama legs
looped over bright sofa armrests

squirming flannel piles entranced by a film.
      A rote boy twists a Trans Am
into a phoenix, verse by hinged verse.

When the doctor asks for questions, he says,
      "Why can't you just put in a new lung?"
That is, *the whole must be preserved*

in all its parts. I clock out. At four
      a.m. it is still raining.
The cocked hammer of a fat drop hits

a window unit. The gutters rush water.
      A thin spout trembles beneath
a waterfall after the world tilts square.

And it tilts square for the baby and brother,
      the mother and the man.
For the lost I think it flows straight up.

See how I twist the flume into a firebird,
      the drops preened like feathers.
The world tilts somewhere for someone,

best to leave hands free for the roller coaster
      I don't want to go anywhere near.
I just want to hear the water

uncontained, taking its own shape,
      sky after sky full of it,
more than a blessing than anything

one drop replacing one drop on the skin
    of a big metal drum,
the outcast maker of phony air.

Loose Ice

To say it's hot is a mistake. Rather
the air is a challenge to move through.
To part it with a gait is to play

a king, the way one feels slapping an ace
on the *pedro,* dropping the deuce
and setting the in-laws back ten.

Call the air wet like the last pass
of a towel, like sweat across
a sunburned neck. Brims sharp,

gas poured into red cans,
Marlboro Reds in square
t-shirt pockets, roustabouts

leaning against a fourteen-foot flat
at the pump, talking across
the island, the counter

spinning, far from lift barges
and pipelines, moping kids
and wives. First a layer

of loose ice, then a six-pack,
another soupy layer, and so on
till the chest snaps shut and

swings into the *caisse,* a shush—
like a priest's to the new kid
when the altar bells shake too long.

Paradis

The land's so flat you can see yesterday
and the years before that. A future
imperceptible behind haze, vespers,
and an oblong sun burning away.

Lacquered greens, virescent, olive, jade,
emerald. Bold brown bark and gray
moss stack up like mile posts,
proof of a coming providence.

The sky should always disappear
on its own, no hills or buildings blocking
its dominance. Spikes of St. Augustine
clasp our feet: There is only *here,*

and then the up, ahead and behind called *there.*
More real than time, it holds us, the portent air.

The Best of Us

Give me your Greek myths
and I'll give you the Carmen

Kief Bridge—forgotten,
whatever it was called before—

where thirty years ago Trey
scaled the steel lift

still hot from the sun of the day,
with a spray can under his chin,

to inscribe the I-beam with the promise
of her memory and the imprimatur of his passion.

Or when Oris G. did his girlfriend on the front lawn
at lunch—I was speechless with admiration.

The football coach looked him right in the eye
and Oris looked right back, the coach hardly

able to draw his smile or keep from pounding Oris
on the back as if he were a safety

just trotting off the field with his first interception.
(What girl could I hold—even under the bleachers?)

      Trey sat with his brother on the T-top
of their Trans Am, a big, wing-stretched

bird stamped in gold on the hood.
They drank the better of a twelve-pack

under the scrawl of a new constellation.
There was no moon, there was no call.

Mr. Kief went to early Mass
with his wife and four daughters,

auburn muses sliding into his car,
one hotter than the next, down to his baby girl,

whose breasts even the straight girls attended.
Did Carmen see the blazón first or did her father,

driving with his neck stretched as if
the crimson letters themselves were suitors

tearing up his sod and eating at his table?
Before the sun set, sandblasters were at work

clouding the message and blotting the sword.
Fathers themselves, they scrubbed

the rust patches and rivets almost to clouds, like those
around great mountain peaks, red rocks

and crags reaching through too-visible haze. "Trey"
watered down to foam by the gritty spray, "loves"

columned in faint streaks, but "Carmen" flaring
like the night it was born from Trey's nozzle.

All that Mr. Kief could not rid himself of:
how his baby became the protagonist,

how she acted through the actor, freeing
herself through photon bonding at the head

of this, our bayou infrastructure. Shame is such
a bastard, its fly-by-night parents,

cowardice and hubris—all that we know
better than God, all we hide from the grass

and the sky. *Her* name will be remembered,
not like a trophy or the blotted girl on the lawn

but like a woman who guards the pass
or a woman who starts a war.

Insufficient, Ineligible Loss

The soft earth between my ribs
    is subsiding.
Nothing grows there.
The strong River carries sewage
    nitrates, sadness
    from thirty-one states.

Memory kills the grass.
    Consciousness kills the fish.
Dramatic, isn't it?
The truth is I'm just depressed
    like everyone else with insufficient loss,
    loss that doesn't kill

But leaves you dissolving
    with the spoil.
Something will take hold
there: a current, a ridge, but
    you won't be around to see,
    you with your view of yesterday.

Travel Slowly Back

"You have a third eye right now," he says to me.

He's standing on Madison, in a flat cap
and half-long scarf, whipping flyers
against the shoulders of passersby,
city-determined and refusing to huff,
much of their faces electrons exploding

like perichoretic atoms in a molecule of water
already feeling themselves liquid or ice
or steaming breath or the pressure exploding

as the three come together unlike any other vehicle
in the universe, any rings on
stars, any powers or principalities,
heights or depths that can separate

the dance of those invisible
single legions of light.

I could see through the synapses of
every face behind him
the way one can see
the bottoms of pools,
the stainless stars.

≈≈

I know you don't believe it, but this is all about you:
about where you went when you saw a stillness
you could not believe, a weight so dry and oppressive
it had to be ironic. Like a boat filling with the water
that once kept it afloat. And then you felt the sails.
And then you felt the whoosh
of the train, the breath of all the conductors
icing at once although it was warm in the car.
Looking through the backwards-running rain,
each house and tree moving you hard. None of these

tropes feels exactly right, your glide from
friend to friend, each mind more transparent
than the last, or the sun off the wet tarmac at 6 a.m.
when you could look right through
to the titanium engines ready to erupt.
Everything smelling like cut grass.

"Life is a circle, turning sometimes right,
sometimes left," he said. "Don't forget
grief has no center, only an apex.
Travel slowly back."

¡Pura Vida!

Let me go, Rafael.

       I've been down here listening
for months as you hand me
one smoking piece of my life then another.

I know letters don't tell the whole story.
You're as good as any MD from the States.

       Better than histology, better than history
you teach me how to peel back a forehead
              and tell me what

I will have to bury, what I will have to love.

You say we're all the same
inside and then show me

something shocking
silver and thin
still firing

or long and binding, scars as fat as fingers.
You love every one of us and carve your great big

Y as if through a tree. Grab my wrist,
Rafael, and pull me onto the cot.

I can't take any more of your sewing lessons.
Wrap your arm around my waist,

twist your legs around what's left.
¡Pura vida! you say. I say, *blow
the fluorescence off my eyes.*

Above *Gasparilla*

    A sudden exuberance
loops
      beyond Neuro's corner room—
a flotilla of pleasure boats
        out the west window, scattered like runes.

A glittering crowd along the sea wall
      bursts into confetti pixels
as the floats move down the bay.

Transfixed, I'm glad
for the five floors between the revelry
and the family, glad no one else sees

more looping scenery
      out the south window
green and purple beads,
red coolers disappearing
      into the southern mansions
        across the bay.

The patient's in here
      flat on a pallet
      like a convertible
in a forties film, not moving,

still chrome-fixed and bright,
      her mouth drawn by a tube
into an odd thespian frown.

Death's downstage for a change.

At a certain point, everyone wants the view from a balcony,
to be spectators rather than revelers,
elbows on railings, all day the same go-cup in hand,
        masked but in no rush to go.

From this fare the west
is endless

the south a short walk up a hill

to a house with rooms as big as
the boats, the boats as big as the bay,

and the man's huge frieze of a face on her thigh
as if she slept the sleep of Endymion,

as if it were already
carnival's Meeting of the Courts

as if she were already that blond adder in a Polo shirt
twining through the crowd with his beer
torched above his head, flushed and laughing

above trumpets and sirens and a wake.

Lauds

Because it was not yet beautiful
Because the light knit the dark
Because sleep was patched with thought

Because the votives were electric
And the chalice was filled with Chablis
Because it was not yet beautiful

Because the light knit the dark
Because the field grass was tipped brown
And the trees fell in spokes

I didn't wake her from the cupboard bed.
I didn't make tea. I didn't
Walk out to the barn with the dog.

I counted on another two hours of sun
To stretch through the clouds. I counted on this life.

Marsh Refrain

The Gulf hums, its waves
rocking and stroking my hair,
varnished, milky, and heavy with salt.

It would part around me if it could,
winding its dials, erasing time.
I list small against the sparkling beige,

a jellyfish, a shell, a tangled line.
I am any and all in its reaches.
My sibling, the trawler, shrinks

to a small button that slips past
the horizon's silver hole. His distance
scares me, and every time he vanishes

I hate him for leaving, his arms raised
in an empty V. Beyond him
a guardrail of rigs I could not hope

to traverse. The waves can never
have me. The map I sent is red
and blue and wrapped in cartilage.

Ode to the Grandiose

The time change
     had me up at dawn, which ordinarily

wouldn't happen. The orchard
       was still soggy, the elk had already been through,
     leaving their little Milk Duds.

I missed out on the bears as well, which you'd
     think would have depressed me,

considering I was up before the bewildering light.

There were piles of apple-dense scat,
     but the hairy goofs hadn't broken a single bough,

the delicate Baldwins still hanging proud
     and innocent. The bears had eaten within

our means and then no doubt napped, each in its lone
     crop circle.

And all the roses I mowed down last year
were twining up even in this dryish fall.

I missed my dog's brisk discoveries,
     but I knew he was with friends
racing his joy at the beach.

I didn't mind the marsh-like stubble;
     in fact, I wrote a couplet in my head,

all iambs—it was fantastic—
      and I counted out the stresses

on my double-front Carhartts
      so I could look woodsy

out in the fields.

It had been cold in the night. Someone
left a window open a notch, and I had hoped

my lover would have a hot flash—
she did not—which was joyous
for her, breathing a merely warm gust
on the sheets, so I could
hardly be disappointed.

The light stretches a different glass everywhere.
The morning just as disjunctive as the night.

I swear I was paying attention
to where the shadows fell,

the songbirds, missing for so
many seasons, chirping chirpy chirps.

And the lady next door, I didn't mind
the unnatural coupling of her horse and donkey.

Aquinas said what is natural for one
can be unnatural for another although

I don't think he was talking about equines.
Mules are blesséd, too.

Something holy descended on the alders,
the green varied and shone and retired

into the shadows, which I was watching
and, for a moment, nothing bad happened anywhere.

Even the loggers were singing for the page
this poem is on.

Embarrassment comes from the word *halter*,
did you know?

A guiding voice helps in a fog, but
with nothing left to burn off,

shake that mane. When you're happy,
it's your prerogative to be grandiose.

Now Hill

See the shadow on the hill, that's now,
and the tall trees in dusky light
on the other side, that must be

where you are: in a future
where strong things keep growing.
Smoke fills my lungs then

dissolves in cold air.
Neither can I hold
a plaited river singing to my ears.

Lying in the Middle of the Field

TIDEWATER, OREGON

The tractor has left rows in the grass,
somewhat like rows of cut cane. Louisiana,
I take you everywhere.

The field itself is a giant row
between aisles of fir and alder,
a chute running west to east,

as I'll run west to east,
not like the hurrying of the sun—
beginning and end being one and all that.

Some might call this loafing.
It is such a pleasure at this point
not to care what the locals

in their trucks, the loggers,
and the UPS man might think
if they saw me from the road.

A field with no boundaries,
an expanse of tideland
is more honest really,

my back sinking in the mud,
high tide covering my joy.

A Chaplet for Lana

I doubt you are quiet even now
    And why should you be

    Now that your voice is unclasped
From the coarse line of our limitations

Your words freed from their pins
    Like white-sleeved spectres

    Caught in a breeze or untangled
From the strophes of your skirt

As you walked unhurried
    Toward a world bent west

    Arriving always
To the chime of fresh things

And what more you can say now
    That every port is yours

Yours our unreachable provinces

In this world one thing passes away so that another may take its place and the whole be preserved in all its parts.

—AUGUSTINE, *Confessions* 4.11

GLOSSARY

Asperges: both the rite of sprinkling holy water as a reminder of baptism and the sprinkler, also known as an aspergillium.

Caisse: (kɛs; Cajun French) truck bed.

Chaplet: a string of beads for prayer; a garland worn as a crown.

Dearfoams: bedroom slippers.

Diener (dē-nər; from the German for servant): the person who runs the morgue.

The Gasparilla Pirate Festival: a celebration of the legend of José Gaspar, a mythical Spanish pirate captain. Members of Ye Mystik Krewe of Gasparilla and a flotilla of hundreds of small boats sail across Tampa Bay, receive the key to the city, and lead a victory parade.

Humeral veil: Roman Catholic liturgical vestment worn across the shoulders.

Igloos: ice chests.

Insufficient, Ineligible Damage (IID): one of FEMA's designations for denied disaster-related claims.

Lookdowns: almost transparent, scythe-like fish found in the Gulf of Mexico.

Meeting of the Courts: the Krewes of Rex and Comus meet at midnight in a ritual marking the end of Mardi Gras.

Pedro (pē-drō): a trick-taking card game as well as the name given the trump that is worth the highest number of points.

St. Augustine: a lawn grass common along the Gulf Coast.

St. Christophers: medals depicting the legend of St. Christopher, who bore Christ on his back while he crossed a river. Christ in turn bore the weight of the world.

Serenity Prayer: prayer for grace, courage, and wisdom attributed to Reinhold Niebuhr and excerpted for wide use by Alcoholics Anonymous.

Starbucks: the largest coffeehouse chain in the world.

Stoup: a vessel for holy water.

Sunshine Bridge: crossing named by Governor Jimmie Davis of Louisiana after the song he composed, "You Are My Sunshine," and which crosses the Mississippi River. For many years after its completion, the south end of the bridge emptied into a swamp. It is rumored the governor had the bridge built for a single supporter who needed sugar cane ferried across the river.

The Way of the Cross: the ritual practice is devotion before a series of pictures that represents scenes in the hours leading up to Jesus' crucifixion. In satirical use, it refers to the practice of stopping at every bar between two points of travel.

ACKNOWLEDGMENTS

I am very grateful to the editors of the following publications in which these poems first appeared:

Birmingham Poetry Review: "Sunshine Bridge"; *Christianity and Literature:* "Insufficient, Ineligible Loss"; *Fogged Clarity:* "Ode to the Grandiose"; *The Hopkins Review:* "Pearl Snap"; *Image: A Journal of the Arts and Religion:* "Asperges" and "*Hirudo Medicinalis*"; *Plume:* "Arrow Boy" and "Free Descent"; *Plume Anthology of Poetry 2013:* "Breakfast at Starbucks with Egret"; *Poetry International:* "Marsh Refrain"; *Prism:* "A Chaplet for Lana"; *Relief:* "Paradis" and "Now Hill"; *St. Katharine's Review:* "The Wild Carp"; *Southern Quarterly Review:* "Above *Gasparilla*" and "White Dog"; *Southwest Review:* "Humus" and "Ten Fathom Ledge"; *The Nation:* "Lying in the Middle of the Field"; *The New Yorker:* "The Best of Us" and "The Diener"; *Vineyards:* "Loose Ice."

≈≈

The collaborative artists' book, *The Diener,* was published by Brighton Press in 2011. This poem appears with etchings and a cast bronze sculpture by Michele Burgess. The limited-edition volume is enclosed in a walnut slipcase.

≈≈

"A Chaplet for Lana" is for Lana's parents, Lilly and Philip Schwebel.

"Travel Slowly Back" is for Lisa Rhoades.

≈≈

My thanks to the chaplains at Tampa General Hospital, especially the 2011–2012 residents, and supervisors Bill Baugh and Wayne Maberry; to my family and friends in Lafourche Parish, Louisiana, who have been so kind during the filming of *Veins in the Gulf,* a documentary by Elizabeth Coffman and Ted Hardin about the State's disappearing wetlands; to generous readers Hayan Charara, Robin Davidson, Pam Diamond, Josh Gottleib-Miller, Joel Hanisek, Fady Judah, Rich Levy, Lynn Randolph, Angela von der Lippe, and Libba Winston; to my editor extraordinaire, Ava Leavell Haymon, and her cadre at LSU; and to Catherine Lenihan and Rochelle St. Marie. My first, last, and best literary critic is Audrey Colombe, who may allow me to pay the debt *ad infinitum.* These poems would not be possible without P., who saved my life and saw for me a more abundant one, and to Rafael Paulino, the diener, who serves the dead with love.

Printed in the USA
CPSIA information can be obtained
at www.ICGtesting.com
LVHW040354220124
769411LV00104B/1101